I0007822

Airtag User Manual and Setup Guide

Simplified Steps for Setting Up and Maximizing Your Airtag with Illustrations

By

Patrick Izzo

Table of Content

INTRODUCTION

Apple has finally introduced AirTag, a compact and elegantly designed device aimed at aiding in the tracking and recovery of misplaced items. This accessory seamlessly integrates with Apple's "Find My" app and can be attached to various items such as bags, keys, or backpacks. AirTag taps into the expansive global network of Apple's "Find My" system, enabling users to pinpoint the location of lost items. Importantly, it maintains the confidentiality and anonymity of location data through robust end-to-end encryption.

In terms of its physical attributes, each AirTag boasts a small and lightweight circular design, meticulously crafted from precision-etched stainless steel. It boasts an IP67 rating, ensuring resilience against water and dust. The device includes a built-in speaker that emits sounds to aid in locating the AirTag and features a removable cover, simplifying battery replacement.

Setting up the AirTag is a straightforward process – users merely need to bring it close to their iPhone, allowing the two devices to establish a connection. Users can then designate AirTags to specific items, assigning default names like "Keys" or "Jacket," or opting for personalized custom names.

Apple has also introduced a range of AirTag accessories, including the Polyurethane Loop, known for its lightweight and durable properties, and the Leather Loop and Leather Key Ring, showcasing tanned European leather. These accessories securely house the AirTag while attaching to the user's belongings, adding a personalized touch to the AirTag experience.

CHAPTER 1

A complete search experience

O nce you've configured your AirTag, it seamlessly integrates into the new Items tab within the Find My app. Users can conveniently access and view the item's real-time or most recently known location on a map within this section. In case a user misplaces their item and remains within Bluetooth range, they can utilize the Find My app to trigger a sound from the AirTag, facilitating the process of locating it. Additionally, users have the option to enlist Siri's assistance in finding their item, with the AirTag responding by emitting a sound if it's in close proximity.

An exceptional feature of every AirTag is the incorporation of the Apple-designed U1 chip, harnessing Ultra Wideband technology. This technology empowers Precision Finding, an exclusive capability accessible to iPhone 11 and iPhone 12 users. Precision Finding represents a groundbreaking leap in locating lost AirTags with remarkable accuracy. It enables users to pinpoint the distance and direction of the AirTag within range. As the user moves, Precision Finding combines data from the device's camera, ARKit, accelerometer, and gyroscope to provide guidance through a combination of auditory, tactile, and visual feedback.

In scenarios where the AirTag has ventured beyond the reach of Bluetooth connectivity, Find My steps to help you track it down. The extensive Where's Network, spanning nearly a billion Apple devices, is poised to assist. It discreetly detects Bluetooth signals from a misplaced AirTag and confidentially conveys its location to the owner. Users can further enhance the search by activating the "lost mode" for the AirTag. This mode ensures they receive notifications when the AirTag reenters Bluetooth range or gets spotted by a device within the vast Where's Network. In the event that a kind soul finds a lost AirTag, they can easily tap it with their iPhone or any NFC-compatible device. This action redirects them to a website that displays a contact phone number for the owner, provided they have chosen to share one. This way, the AirTag serves as a communal tool for reuniting lost items with their owners, promoting privacy and efficiency.

Integrated privacy and security

When you set up your AirTag, it's like giving your lost item to a guardian. You'll find your AirTag in the "Items" tab of the Find My app, where you can easily check out its current or last known location on a map. And if your item goes missing while it's within Bluetooth range, you can ask the Find My app to play a sound on your AirTag to help you track it down. Siri can also lend a hand – ask her to find your item, and the AirTag will make a sound if it's nearby.

The cool thing about AirTag is that it packs an Apple-designed U1 chip, using Ultra Wideband technology. As you move around, your phone combines camera info, ARKit, accelerometer, and gyroscope data to guide you with sounds, vibrations, and visuals to lead you straight to your AirTag.

But what if your AirTag goes out of Bluetooth range? No worries, the Find My app has your back. Thanks to the extensive Where's Network, made up of nearly a billion Apple devices, it can catch Bluetooth signals from your lost AirTag and quietly let you know where it's hiding, all while keeping everything anonymous and private.

You can even put your AirTag in "lost mode." This way, you'll get notifications when it's in range or if it gets spotted by another device in the Where's Network. And if someone kind finds your lost AirTag, they can tap it with their iPhone or an NFC-compatible device, and they'll be directed to a website that shows your contact phone number if you've shared one.

What exactly are AirTags?

The AirTag, a revolutionary Bluetooth tracker, offers an ingenious solution for safeguarding personal belongings. Its compact size, roughly like a coin, grants you the flexibility to attach it to a wide array of items effortlessly. For instance, consider attaching it to your keys; should these keys venture beyond a designated distance from your paired iPhone, your phone will promptly emit an alert, drawing your attention to the potential loss.

In the event that you miss this initial warning, fear not, for AirTag provides a step-by-step guide within the iPhone's "Find My" feature, enabling you to pinpoint the exact location of your misplaced keys. In essence, the AirTag functions as a Bluetooth location tracker par excellence, granting you the power to secure your cherished possessions. From your iPad to your wallet, keys, and handbag, affix an AirTag, and you can trace your items via the "Find My" feature on your iPhone.

Now, let's jump right into the inner workings of the AirTag. This cutting-edge device boasts a built-in UWB (Ultra-Wideband) chip, synergizing seamlessly with iPhone 11 and iPhone 12 models equipped with the U1 ultra-wideband radio chip. UWB technology leverages ultra-narrow pulses, delivering high transmission rates, low transmit power, and exceptional penetration capabilities. This technological synergy enables iPhones to track AirTags with ultra-wideband technology with unparalleled precision.

Recent updates in iOS 14.3 have further streamlined the user experience. You can now enter "findmy://items" in Safari to swiftly access the search application and navigate to the AirTag setting interface. You can effortlessly add items that require tracking, binding them to the AirTag. If any of these items wander beyond your reach, your iPhone will notify you promptly. With a quick tap within the "Find My App," the AirTag emits a loud, unmistakable beep, aiding in the swift recovery of your misplaced possessions.

The AirTag, with its impressive utility, is poised to become a lifesaver for those prone to forgetfulness. With an estimated price point of approximately $25, this innovation promises to be accessible to a wide audience. Notably, accessory manufacturers have already begun producing protective covers for AirTags, enhancing their durability and functionality.

Currently, AirTag compatibility extends to iPhone 11 and iPhone 12 models, offering users an unparalleled tracking experience. In summary, the AirTag's primary purpose is straightforward: it is a small, Bluetooth-enabled device empowered by UWB technology, designed to assist in locating objects through the use of an iPad or iPhone. While similar products exist, Apple's AirTag sets a new standard for precision and ease of use, promising redefining how we track our treasured belongings.

AirTags design

The AirTag is a button-shaped tracking device with a pristine white exterior. Its front-facing design allows for customization through engravings and the addition of silver accents, offering users a touch of personalization. Designed to be powered by a CR2032 internal battery, the AirTag necessitates the use of supplementary accessories for establishing a connection with the desired item.

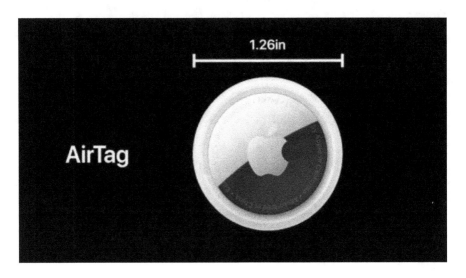

In terms of physical dimensions, this compact marvel measures 1.26 inches in width and 0.31 inches in height, equating to approximately 8 millimeters. Despite its impressive tracking capabilities, it remains incredibly lightweight, tipping the scales at a mere 0.39 ounces, which is roughly equivalent to 11 grams. This combination of design, functionality, and portability makes the AirTag an invaluable tool for tracking and safeguarding your belongings.

AirTag recording

Every individual AirTag possesses the capability to encode a maximum of four characters, whether they are alphanumeric or emoji characters. Nevertheless, it is important to acknowledge that the inherent constraints of AirTag's compact form factor impose certain restrictions, particularly when using emojis. Moreover, Apple has implemented stringent content filtering mechanisms, prohibiting specific emoji combinations and phrases to maintain a respectful and responsible user experience.

To provide a concrete illustration of these restrictions, consider that it is not permissible to pair emojis such as the "horse face" and the "poop" emoji within the content of an AirTag. Furthermore, using offensive or profane language in any form is strictly forbidden within the confines of AirTag's encoding capabilities, aligning with Apple's commitment to fostering a wholesome and user-friendly digital environment. These measures ensure that the AirTag remains a device that upholds the values of respect and propriety while offering its innovative tracking capabilities.

AirTags activity

The integration of AirTag into the "Find My" program, a feature introduced by Apple as of iOS 14.3, has greatly expanded the capabilities and management options for this cutting-edge tracking device. Within the "Find My" program, you can seamlessly add and oversee your AirTag, conveniently located under the dedicated "Item" tab.

Like other esteemed Apple devices, each AirTag is prominently displayed within the "Find My" app, enabling you to keep tabs on its whereabouts effortlessly. These AirTags establish Bluetooth connections with your iOS and macOS devices, ensuring constant accessibility.

A standout feature of the AirTag is the incorporation of the U1 chip, which elevates tracking precision to an unprecedented level. Whether your AirTag is nestled within the confines of your home or placed outside, even when not nearby, the U1 chip empowers you to pinpoint its exact location with remarkable accuracy. Should your AirTag ever go missing within your own domicile, there's no need to fret, as a built-in audio player comes to the rescue. You have the option to activate this feature through the "Find My" program, or simply enlist Siri's assistance in locating the audible beacon emitted by the AirTag.

In the unfortunate event that your AirTag becomes lost or stolen, the "Find My" network steps in as a reliable ally in the quest for its recovery. Leveraging the collective strength of hundreds of millions of iPhone, iPad, and Mac devices worldwide, the "Find My Network" forms a formidable alliance to help you locate your AirTag. When someone else's device detects an AirTag, its location is promptly displayed on a map, facilitating a swift and efficient retrieval process.

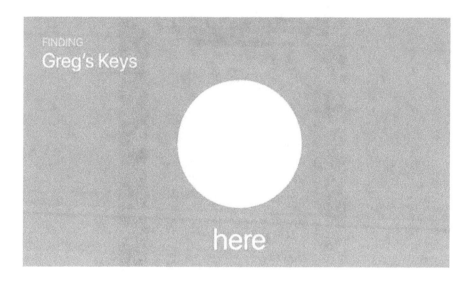

Furthermore, "Lost Mode" adds an extra layer of protection. Should a kind soul within the "People Who Found Me" network stumble upon your AirTag, it automatically triggers a notification. You have the option to include your contact details, ensuring that the individual who has found your item can easily get in touch with you. AirTag and the "Find My" program form a robust ecosystem that seamlessly combines advanced technology, user-friendly features, and a global network of devices to safeguard and recover your cherished belongings.

Accurate search

For iPhone users fortunate enough to possess a device equipped with the U1 chip, such as the iPhone 11 and iPhone 12 models, there's a remarkable feature at their disposal known as Precision Finding. This cutting-edge functionality elevates the experience of retrieving a misplaced AirTag to an entirely new level.

Precision Finding enables you to access detailed, step-by-step instructions on locating and recovering your lost AirTag with pinpoint accuracy. It does this through a combination of advanced technologies, including augmented reality (AR), audible sound cues, and tactile touch feedback. This multi-faceted approach enhances the precision and effectiveness of the search process, ensuring that you can swiftly and confidently reclaim your valuable belongings.

In essence, Precision Finding represents a fusion of innovative technology and user-centric design, harnessing the power of the U1 chip to provide an unparalleled tracking experience for iPhone users, thereby reaffirming Apple's commitment to enhancing the utility and convenience of its ecosystem.

Replace missing AirTag

When you encounter a lost AirTag, or if someone else stumbles upon one, a straightforward and thoughtful solution is at your disposal. You can use any NFC-equipped smartphone, whether it runs on iPhone or Android, to initiate a scan of the AirTag. This simple action will reveal the owner's contact details, allowing you to take the appropriate steps to return the lost item to its rightful owner.

Moreover, if the AirTag happens to be in "Lost" mode, it employs a clever mechanism to further aid in its recovery. In this mode, the AirTag leverages the power of the "Find My" network to transmit its location information back to the owner periodically. This innovative feature ensures that the owner remains updated with the AirTag's whereabouts, facilitating a smoother and more efficient retrieval process. AirTag's combination of NFC scanning and "Lost" mode functionality represents a powerful duo, enabling the device to fulfill its mission of reuniting lost items with their owners.

AirTags battery

AirTags are equipped with a CR2032 battery that is integrated and non-removable for the convenience of users. This durable battery has been designed to provide reliable power for up to a full year before requiring replacement. When the time comes to replace the battery, the process is user-friendly and straightforward.

To replace the battery in your AirTag, you can press and twist the device's back panel. This action allows you to easily access and replace the CR2032 battery, ensuring that your AirTag can continue its valuable tracking functions. Additionally, you won't have to worry about monitoring the battery life constantly, as the AirTag itself will notify you when the battery is running low, prompting you to take the necessary steps to keep your tracking device operating at its best. This user-centric approach ensures that maintaining the functionality of your AirTag remains hassle-free and efficient.

AirTag charging

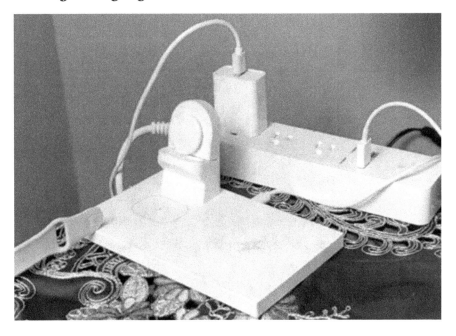

AirTag, a testament to Apple's thoughtful engineering, eliminates the perennial hassle of constant charging. This convenience is made possible by the clever design choice of utilizing CR2032 batteries, which provide reliable power and offer the user the ability to replace them as needed. It means you can wave goodbye to the anxiety of running out of charge and instead focus on the peace of mind that comes with a tracking device that's always ready for action.

AirTags Range

In its typical fashion of prioritizing user experience, Apple hasn't left users in the dark regarding AirTag's range capabilities. While precise specifics might be a closely guarded secret, it is common knowledge that AirTag boasts a robust Bluetooth range extending to approximately 100 meters.

This generous range opens up a world of possibilities for tracking your belongings, whether they're in close proximity or a bit farther away. However, for those who crave more in-depth insights into AirTag's range performance, undertaking additional testing might be the key to unlocking its full potential.

AirTags Water Resistance

In the realm of durability, AirTag proudly flaunts an impressive IP67 rating for waterproofing and dust resistance. This certification is not just a fancy badge; it signifies that AirTag can confidently withstand immersion in water for up to 30 minutes at a depth of one meter (equivalent to approximately 3.3 feet) under carefully controlled laboratory conditions.

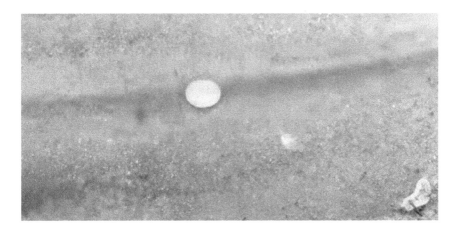

This level of ruggedness ensures that AirTag remains unfazed by encounters with rainwater or the occasional accidental spillage, guaranteeing its reliability even in the face of the elements.

AirTags Settings

When it comes to setting up your AirTag, Apple has streamlined the process to perfection, mirroring the effortless experience you might have encountered with AirPods. When you unbox your AirTag, a single tap is all it takes to configure the device, putting you on the fast track to track your valuables. But the customization doesn't stop there. AirTag's versatility extends to the realm of personalization, where you have the freedom to give each one a unique name and description, adding an extra layer of organization and personal touch to your tracking experience.

AirTag ID Restrictions

Apple understands that life can be dynamic filled with countless items that need monitoring and protection. That's why they've generously allowed each Apple ID to be associated with up to a staggering 16 AirTags at once.

It means you can effortlessly keep tabs on a multitude of items simultaneously, from the smallest valuables to the most significant possessions. This adaptability ensures that AirTag can cater to your specific tracking needs, whether you're safeguarding a handful of treasured belongings or managing a comprehensive inventory of items with ease.

AirTags privacy and security

Each and every AirTag within your possession is intricately linked to your individual "Apple ID," establishing an impenetrable connection that precludes anyone else from monitoring its movements. This exclusive association guarantees that your AirTag experience remains a private and personalized endeavor, impervious to external tracking attempts.

An essential facet of AirTag's privacy architecture revolves around refraining from retaining any location data or historical location logs. This deliberate omission ensures that your past journeys and those of your belongings remain shrouded in confidentiality, shielded from prying eyes.

Furthermore, when devices collaborate to transmit the location of a lost AirTag, they do so while preserving the utmost anonymity. At each juncture of this transmission, the location data is meticulously shrouded in encryption, safeguarding the privacy of those involved. Even in the event that someone else's device discovers your AirTag, you, as the rightful owner, maintain the privilege of glimpsing its location on a map. However, this does not compromise the anonymity of the person who contributed to its retrieval. Apple's steadfast commitment to end-to-end encryption extends to the point where not even Apple itself possesses access to the location data of your AirTag.

In addition to these robust privacy measures, AirTag boasts a dynamic Bluetooth identifier that is in perpetual rotation. This ingenious feature guarantees that your AirTag or any comparable tracking device cannot maintain a persistent trail of your movements. It acts as an indomitable safeguard, assuring that your personal space and privacy remain inviolate.

In essence, AirTag is a paragon of privacy-centric design, where each element of its operation is calibrated to protect your confidentiality and security. Your "Apple ID" serves as an unbreakable shield against external tracking, while the absence of location data storage ensures that your past movements remain your own. Anonymity is preserved through encryption, offering you the convenience of tracking without compromising your privacy. The rotating Bluetooth identifier adds an extra layer of security, reinforcing your peace of mind. In this intricate tapestry of privacy features, AirTag embodies Apple's unwavering commitment to safeguarding your personal space and data.

Unwanted tracking restrictions

Apple's commitment to privacy and security extends to implementing robust measures within AirTag to prevent its misuse for unwarranted privacy invasions.

In scenarios where another AirTag, belonging to someone else, unexpectedly appears in your vicinity and accompanies you for an extended period, your trusty iPhone will serve as a vigilant guardian. It will promptly dispatch an alert to notify you of the presence of an AirTag detected nearby, thereby thwarting any inadvertent tracking attempts. This proactive notification ensures that your personal privacy remains intact, bolstering your peace of mind.

Moreover, upon your return to your home address or frequently visited locations, your iPhone will issue a distinctive "AirTag Found" warning. It further enhances your awareness and safeguards your privacy. This warning mechanism empowers you with the ability to take immediate action, such as disabling the AirTag in question, ensuring that you retain control over your tracking experience.

When you receive these notifications, you have the option to tap on them to swiftly disable the detected AirTag, putting you in charge of your privacy. Suppose you are utilizing an AirTag on an item intended for temporary borrowing. In that case, you can opt to turn off the one-day "AirTag Detected" notification, offering enhanced flexibility in tailoring your tracking experience to your specific needs.

Additionally, for family members within your "Family Sharing" group, you have the capability to customize "Security Notifications," allowing you to fine-tune your privacy preferences. This comprehensive suite of security features underscores Apple's dedication to providing users with a robust, customizable, and privacy-first tracking experience. It empowers you to take control of your privacy while enjoying the benefits of AirTag's tracking capabilities with the utmost confidence.

How to turn off anonymous AirTags that are available to you to prevent tracking

The AirTag notification you receive is designed to be applicable only when the AirTag has been distinctly separated from its rightful owner. This thoughtful design ensures that you can avoid receiving unwarranted alerts due to the presence of friends or family members who happen to have their own AirTags in close proximity. Your privacy and peace of mind are safeguarded, as the AirTag's alert system remains focused on situations where it genuinely matters.

Furthermore, when an AirTag has been away from its owner for a continuous duration of three days, it exhibits a clever self-reminder mechanism. In this scenario, the AirTag emits an audible noise each time it departs from its current location. This auditory cue serves as a reminder of its presence and existence, assisting in preventing unintentional separations and contributing to the device's overall effectiveness in safeguarding your belongings. This innovative feature underscores AirTag's commitment to enhancing your tracking experience while ensuring privacy and convenience are always at the forefront.

CHAPTER 2

How to replace AirTag battery

The AirTag runs on CR2032 button-shaped batteries, which have an impressive lifespan of approximately one year before they require replacement. Now, there's currently no immediate need to replace the battery, but should the time come when you do, the process is straightforward and hassle-free.

These CR2032 batteries are readily available as standard options and can be conveniently purchased on popular platforms like Amazon. They typically cost around $1 each and are also stocked in most general stores for your convenience.

Once you have your new battery in hand, follow these easy steps for replacement:

1. Begin by pressing the stainless steel support on your AirTag.

2. With the support pressed, give it a counterclockwise twist until the lid stops turning.

3. It will effectively separate the two halves of the AirTag.

4. Carefully remove the old battery.

5. Insert the new one in the same orientation, ensuring it faces upwards. Once the battery is securely in place, you'll hear a reassuring sound to confirm it's properly seated.

To monitor your AirTag's battery status, simply check the "Find My" app. It will provide you with updates, and when the battery starts running low, you'll receive a notification on your iPhone, signaling that it's time for a battery replacement. This user-friendly approach ensures that maintaining your AirTag's functionality remains a straightforward and worry-free experience.

How to install AirTag on iPhone

Apple AirTag is a small button-built tool designed to link to items such as keys and wallets so that these apps can be hunted down using Apple-enabled Bluetooth on Apple's "Find Me" app.

If you have a new AirTag, you must set it up and configure it. Before performing this operation, please update your iPhone or iPad to iOS 14.5 or iPadOS 14.5, respectively. You can check

your iOS version in Settings -> General -> Software Updates.
->

How to install AirTag on iPhone and iPad

1. Ensure that your iPhone is powered on and displaying the home screen.
2. If there's a protective battery label on your AirTag, remove it and bring the AirTag closer to your iPhone.

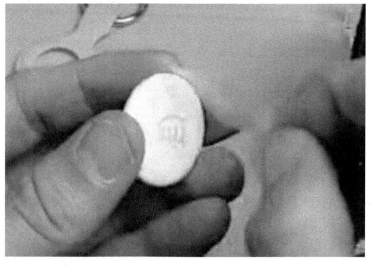

3. On the card on your screen, tap the "Connect" option.

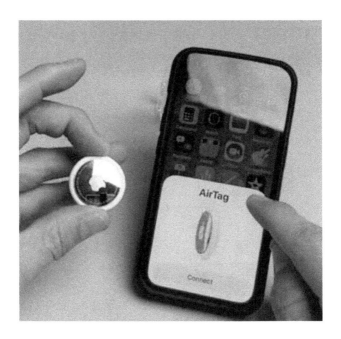

4. You'll be presented with a list of names to choose from, or if you prefer, you can select "Custom Name" to enter a unique name and even choose an emoji to personalize it. Afterward, tap "Continue."

5. Proceed by tapping "Continue" to register the item to your Apple ID, and then wrap things up by clicking "Done."

CHAPTER 3

The Application

At the heart of this sophisticated system lies the "Find My" application, a cornerstone of iOS. It is primarily known for its ability to locate Apple devices such as the iPhone, iPad, Apple Watch, and Mac. Within this application is where we discover the indispensable AirTags, seamlessly integrated with items we hold dear and intend not to misplace. The interface and functionality will feel like second nature for those familiar with other Apple products.

In the past, there were compelling discussions about an "augmented reality" mode that would have allowed us to visually pinpoint the precise location of an AirTag through the iPhone's screen. The notion that we could peer through our iPhone camera, frame our surroundings, and visually identify our lost item seemed almost like magic. However, as of now, this promising feature has yet to materialize fully. Hints of this functionality have surfaced within iOS 3's code, with cryptic instructions suggesting to "walk a few meters and move your iPhone up and down until you see a balloon." While this remains a tantalizing glimpse into the potential future of AirTags, it remains to be seen if and when this feature will become a reality.

We can assert with certainty that in the days ahead, even third-party manufacturers will be able to integrate their devices into the "Find My" network. A clear indication of this shift occurred recently when a certification program was unveiled, allowing non-Apple devices to become part of the "Find My" ecosystem. Similar to the esteemed "Made for iPhone" (MFi) certification, these compatible products will need Apple's approval, provided they adhere to specific criteria. These criteria encompass sound power levels, NFC technology capabilities, firmware standards, Bluetooth connectivity, and, notably, UWB (Ultra-Wideband) technology, a game-changing innovation that sets AirTag apart from any other tracking product currently available on the market.

As we look to the future, it's a promising landscape for the "Find My" network and AirTags alike. The potential for augmented reality features looms on the horizon, and the prospect of third-party integration heralds an exciting era of expanded compatibility, ultimately amplifying the utility of these remarkable tracking devices.

Lost "community" mode

When a device finds itself beyond the range of an AirTag and the associated iPhone, an ingenious mechanism known as the "community lost mode" is set into motion. This mode is designed to harness the collective power of iPhone users to assist in recovering lost items. Here's how it works: Whenever any individual with an iPhone ventures close to an item marked by an AirTag, the owner of that AirTag gains valuable insights into its precise location. If the AirTag is currently in "lost mode," a notification will alert the owner, indicating that their AirTag is nearby and may have been misplaced.

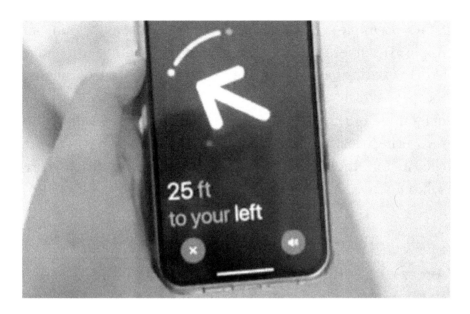

At this juncture, a user who comes close to the lost AirTag, armed with an iPhone or another NFC-equipped device, can access a dedicated website. This website serves as a vital hub, providing a means to establish contact with individuals who have misplaced their AirTag, even if they are hundreds or thousands of kilometers away.

Some of Apple's flagship technologies, such as iCloud and Apple ID, underpin this remarkable functionality. It operates akin to existing location features in devices like Tile, harnessing the power of a vast community of iPhone users. The sheer magnitude of iPhone users greatly enhances the likelihood of recovering a lost AirTag-equipped item, making it a compelling choice for those seeking reliable and efficient tracking solutions.

Found by anyone who does not have an iPhone

AirTags exhibit this remarkable behavior by emitting a distinct ringing sound when moved, serving as a clever, attention-grabbing mechanism. Currently, this activation occurs after three days has passed since separation from the owner. However, it's worth noting that Apple can adjust this timeframe through a simple software update, ensuring that AirTags remain finely tuned to user preferences.

What's particularly intriguing is that even when an AirTag falls into the hands of an individual who doesn't own an iPhone, it's still possible to ascertain the rightful owner. A smartphone is required with NFC (Near Field Communication) technology. This innovative feature underscores the AirTag's versatility and commitment to ensuring that lost items find their way back to their owners, regardless of the device in the hands of the person who discovers them.

Privacy function

In light of this advanced technology, it's entirely understandable for individuals to harbor concerns regarding safeguarding their personal data. However, Apple has meticulously architected the entire system with the utmost commitment to privacy protection. Apple elucidates that within the accessory itself, no data about its gradual locations is absent. The communication with the Dov'è network occurs through an encrypted protocol, ensuring the utmost security. Furthermore, access to this data is restricted exclusively to those in possession of the Airtag, thereby preserving the privacy of its users.

It's imperative to note that even individuals who engage in the crowdsourcing network aimed at assisting in the retrieval of a misplaced Airtag remain unaware of their contribution to the device's location. Only in instances where the rightful owner activates the Airtag's "lost mode" does the possibility of retrieving information through an NFC device, such as an iPhone or another compatible phone (including Android devices), come into play. An internet page is summoned at this juncture, granting access to the Airtag's serial number and potentially the owner's phone number if it has been shared. Even Apple needs to be made aware of the whereabouts of the individual devices it assists in tracking. A meticulously designed system has been implemented throughout the development process, systematically rotating Bluetooth signal identifiers to preempt any interception attempts.

Anti-stalker function

To grasp the significance of this feature, consider the unsettling scenario where individuals with ulterior motives attempt to track someone's movements using the tracker secretly. Apple has taken measures to thwart such actions, introducing a layer of complexity to this dubious pursuit.

Here's how it works: If we happen to have an Airtag that doesn't belong to us, a notification is promptly dispatched to our iPhone, bearing a concise yet potent message: "A found Airtag is moving with you." This notification materializes under two specific conditions—either the Airtag isn't paired with our iPhone, or there's no Airtag with an iPhone nearby. This intelligent design mitigates the risk of receiving notifications from devices belonging to individuals sharing, for example, the same train compartment.

Upon receiving this notification, users have the power to take immediate action. By simply tapping on the notification, they can trigger the Airtag to emit a distinct ringing sound. This auditory cue serves as an invaluable aid in promptly locating the Airtag, thereby preventing any unwanted surveillance and safeguarding personal privacy.

Precise Position Function

When an Airtag goes astray, the potential to pinpoint its whereabouts becomes a reality through a rather nifty feature— following an auditory trail. As one draws closer to the misplaced Airtag or orients themselves in the correct direction,

the volume of sound emitted gradually escalates, effectively guiding the user towards the target. Conversely, stepping away or turning in another direction causes this sound to diminish, aiding in the process of relocating the Airtag. This ingenious functionality is aptly christened "Precise Position" and is made feasible by incorporating the U1 chip, the Ultra-Wideband (UWB) technology bedrock.

This very same U1 chip, in synergy with a medley of technologies and components, including ARKit, accelerometers, and gyroscopes, culminates in remarkable accuracy when tracking Airtags. The workings of this component may ring familiar to owners of iPhone 11 (where it made its debut) or iPhone 12 devices, particularly when initiating an AirDrop. On such occasions, the phone adeptly discerns the direction it should be oriented towards, courtesy of the UWB chip's exceptional "spatial awareness." Thanks to this technology, the precision of locating objects is dialed in at an impressive 30 centimeters, rendering it the ideal tool for retrieving misplaced items. It's worth noting that Airtags are also compatible with older iPhones; however, the Precise Location mode remains inactive when used with devices lacking the UWB capability, which is a distinguishing feature of iPhone 11 and iPhone 12 models.

The Airtag battery

There was debate about the Airtag's battery, with most rumors suggesting using a CR2032 battery. These speculations were accurate, and indeed, the Airtag utilizes a CR2032 battery, which is widely available at an affordable price (even less than one euro each on Amazon). Replacing the battery is a straightforward process that the end-user can perform without needing special tools or skills.

Accessories for Airtag

Apple offers additional accessories for the Airtag, such as key rings designed to attach the Airtag to objects you wish to track securely. However, it's important to note that these accessories are not included in the Airtag's initial purchase and must be acquired separately. Apple's accessory lineup currently includes a leather keychain and two lanyards, one made of leather and the other crafted from silicone.

Apple Airtag accessories

1. Apple offers exclusive Hermes pendants, luggage tags, and key rings bundled with personalized Airtags. However, these options are on the higher end of the price spectrum, ranging from 299 to 449 euros.
2. For more budget-friendly alternatives, Belkin provides Airtag accessories priced at 14 euros, offering a cost-effective choice.
3. If you explore Amazon, you'll find many similar Airtag accessories with prices starting at less than ten euros and going up to 20 euros. These may not match the premium quality of Apple or Belkin offerings, but provide affordable options.

4. The Nomad eyeglass strap is an intriguing and innovative choice to accommodate an Airtag. This accessory caters to those who wear glasses, providing an inventive way to keep track of eyewear.

Here are some examples of accessory prices at the time of this writing:

- Airtag silicone strap (available in various colors): 35 euros.
- Airtag leather keychain: 39 euros.
- Airtag leather strap: 45 euros.

These accessory options cater to various preferences and budgets, ensuring Airtag users have various choices to suit their needs.

Linking Airtags to Your Device

If you've recently acquired an Apple AirTag and need guidance on installing it, worry not! Linking an AirTag to your iPhone or iPad is a breeze, akin to pairing a new AirPods with your Apple account. Here's a step-by-step breakdown of the process:

1. Commence by unboxing the AirTag and gently removing the protective plastic. As you do so, the AirTag will emit a brief beep.

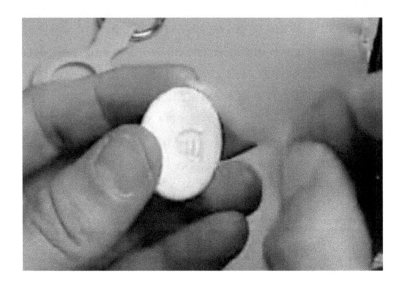

2. Next, position the AirTag within proximity, mere inches, of your unlocked iPhone or iPad running iOS 14.5, iPadOS 14.5, or a later version. Your mobile device should promptly detect the presence of the Bluetooth tracker.

3. When a popup message materializes on your screen, seize the opportunity to tap the "Connect" button.

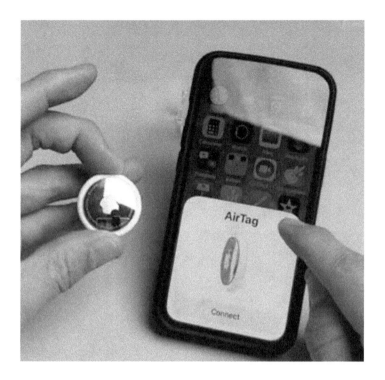

4. If, by any chance, the on-screen dialog fails to make an appearance within a few seconds, take the following steps: lock your iPhone or iPad, unlock it once more, and maneuver the AirTag nearer to the Side/Power button.

5. At this point, you can give a name to your AirTag that corresponds with the item you intend to track using this accessory. If none of the default names align with your purpose, the "Custom Name" option is available.

6. Click on the "Continue" button to proceed.

7. Pick a suitable name and confirm your selection.
8. The popup message displays the email address and phone number linked to your Apple ID. These details will be associated with your AirTag, should it ever get misplaced and someone attempts to identify the owner.
9. Tap "Continue" to complete the registration of the AirTag on your Apple ID.
10. Click on the "Continue" button to proceed.
11. Pick a suitable name and confirm your selection.
12. The popup message displays the email address and phone number linked to your Apple ID. These details will be associated with your AirTag, should it ever get misplaced and someone attempts to identify the owner.

46

13. Tap "Continue" to complete the registration of the AirTag on your Apple ID.

14. The configuration of your AirTag is now complete. Allow a minute or two for the setup to finalize. Please be patient while the AirTag completes the installation process.

15. Your AirTag is now successfully connected to your iPhone or iPad and has been added to the Find My Network.

16. Alternatively, you can choose the "Done" link to complete the installation.

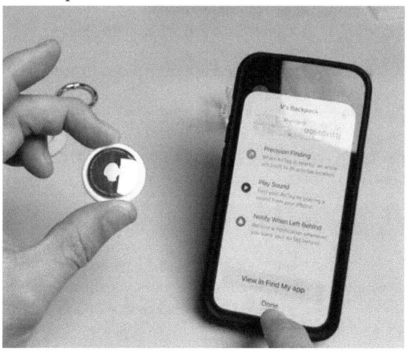

In the Find My app, you'll find a real-time map displaying the AirTag's location (if it's within Bluetooth range of an iPhone, iPad, or Mac). You'll also find a button to activate audio playback through the tracker and a "Search" option to pinpoint the accessory precisely, provided your iPhone has a U1 chip (iPhone 11 and later). You can also mark the AirTag as lost, change its name, or remove the Bluetooth tracker from your Apple ID and the Find My Network.

In the future, you can revisit this page by launching the Find My app on your iPhone or iPad. Alternatively, if you can't locate it on your device, you can swiftly locate the app using Spotlight Search. The configuration of your AirTag is now complete. Allow a minute or two for the setup to finalize. Please be patient while the AirTag completes the installation process.

How to Put an AirTag in Lost Mode

The Apple AirTag is a compact, coin-sized device designed to be attached to items like keys and wallets. It lets you track these belongings within the "Find My" app through a Bluetooth connection with your nearby Apple device.

Lost Mode

To monitor the whereabouts of your AirTags, access the "Items" tab within the "Find My Items" section, a feature designed to provide a tracking experience similar to that of Apple devices. In the unfortunate event that an AirTag goes missing, you can activate "Lost Mode," a feature aimed at expediting its recovery.

When an AirTag is close to an Apple device, it swiftly establishes a Bluetooth connection, facilitating the seamless sharing of its exact location. An additional layer of functionality comes into play for users of iPhone 11 and 12 models. Thanks to the sophisticated U1 chip, these devices feature a specialized direct search function. This function proves invaluable for pinpointing items that have been mistakenly placed nearby.

But what if an AirTag strays beyond the immediate reach of your device's Bluetooth signal? Rest assured, the "Find My" app remains an indispensable tool. In such scenarios, it doesn't solely rely on your device's Bluetooth signals. Instead, it harnesses the expansive "Find My" network, an extensive web comprising nearly a million Apple devices globally. These devices join forces to come to your aid, ensuring that your AirTag and the attached item remain within your grasp.

Nonetheless, if an AirTag finds itself quite a distance away from your location, and there are no Apple devices in its immediate vicinity, "Find My" will provide the last known location on the map. In such instances, you still possess the capability to activate "Lost Mode," a beacon of hope in the quest to recover your lost item. By doing so, should a Good Samaritan with an NFC-enabled or Android device come across your lost AirTag, it can be crucial in facilitating its safe return. It is the ingenious system in action, ensuring that your cherished belongings are always within reach.

AirTag Lost Mode function

AirTags offers a highly convenient tracking solution accessible through the "Articles" tab within the Find My app. Similar to Apple devices, should an AirTag ever go astray, you can engage "Lost Mode" – a powerful tool to retrieve your lost item.

When an AirTag finds itself near an Apple device, it swiftly establishes a Bluetooth connection, enabling seamless sharing of its precise location. An additional feature comes into play for owners of iPhone 11 and 12 models. Thanks to the advanced U1 chip, these devices boast a precision location feature. This feature proves immensely helpful when tracking down items inadvertently misplaced nearby.

But what if an AirTag ventures beyond the reach of your device's Bluetooth signal? Fret not, for the Find My app remains at your service. The app doesn't rely on your device's Bluetooth signals in this scenario. Instead, it harnesses the vast "Find My" network, a colossal conglomerate comprising nearly a billion Apple devices dispersed globally. These devices work in unison to aid you, ensuring your AirTag and the attached item are always within reach.

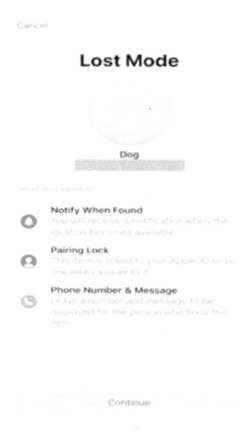

Lost Mode

Dog

Notify When Found
You will receive a notification when the location becomes available

Pairing Lock
This item is linked to your Apple ID so no one else can pair to it

Phone Number & Message
Leave a number and message to be displayed for the person who finds this item

Continue

So, even when your AirTag finds itself far from home, without any nearby Apple devices, "Find My" has your back by providing the last known location on the map. In such cases, you retain the ability to activate "Lost Mode," a safeguard that can be a beacon of hope. By doing so, if a Good Samaritan with an NFC-enabled or Android device stumbles upon your lost AirTag, it can play a pivotal role in its safe return to you. It is the ingenious system designed to ensure that your belongings are never truly lost.

Airtag notification

In scenarios where an AirTag finds itself distant from your location, and no Apple devices are in its immediate vicinity, Find My can only provide the last known location on the map.

However, there's a valuable recourse in such cases – activating "Lost Mode." This feature allows someone with an iPhone or Android device equipped with NFC to interact with the AirTag and assist in its safe return. Here's a breakdown of how this ingenious system works.

How to mark an AirTag as lost

1. Open the Find My app on your iPhone.

2. Tap on "Items" to access your AirTags.

3. Select the specific AirTag you want to mark as lost.
4. Scroll down on the map view and tap "Activate Lost Mode" under the Lost Mode section for the chosen AirTag.

5. Tap "Continue."

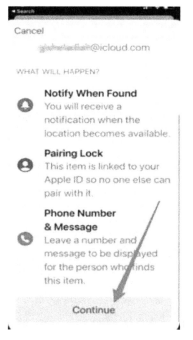

6. In the input field, enter a phone number where you can be reached, and then tap "Next."

7. Enable the switch next to "Notify me when found." Optionally, you can customize the message appearing when someone finds the object. Please note that message customization and "Notify me when found" are only available if the AirTag is out of range of your device.
8. Tap "Activate."

Once you've marked the AirTag as lost, a notification will appear containing a website URL if someone discovers it and brings it near an NFC-enabled iPhone or Android phone. This URL will lead to a webpage displaying the customized lost message and the provided phone number. Thanks to the Find My Network, you may also have the chance to view the shared location via another person's device, potentially aiding in recovering your lost item.

How to Easily Rename Airtag and Change Its Emoji

If you've recently acquired Apple's latest item tracking accessory, you'll be pleased to know that customization options are available. While some customization choices can be made during the ordering process or with the selection of accessories, the real scope for personalization lies within the software. Apple has thoughtfully provided the means to rename your AirTag and even alter its associated emoji, allowing for a more accurate representation of the item it's intended to keep tabs on.

Before getting into the details of how to rename your AirTag and change its emoji, it's worth noting that during the initial setup, you can assign a default name to Apple's item tracking accessory. However, should you ever wish to modify the name or emoji, the Find My app offers the flexibility to do so at your convenience. It becomes particularly relevant when you decide to forego using cases or want a fresh perspective.

For those unfamiliar with the process, here are step-by-step instructions on how to rename your AirTag and change its associated emoji:

1. Open the Find My app on your device.

2. Navigate to the "Items" tab within the app.

Items

🙂 **okay** 📍 i am okay
▪▪▪ · 7 minutes ago

🎒 **peter's Backpack**
▪▪▪ · 7 minutes ago

+ Add New Item

3. Identify the AirTag you wish to rename and select it.
4. Scroll down to locate and tap on the 'Rename Item' option.

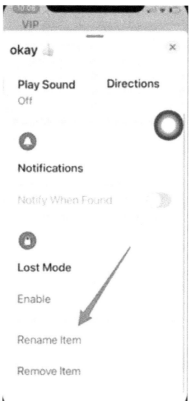

5. Enter the New Name you'd like to assign to your AirTag.
6. Confirm your changes by tapping 'Done.'

How to Remove AirTag from Your Apple ID Account Before Selling It

The AirTag is an incredibly handy accessory that can be affixed to your belongings to keep track of their whereabouts. Recently unveiled at Apple's Spring Loaded event, the AirTag is available for purchase at a price of $29 each. Additionally, you can acquire a four-pack for $99, providing you with some cost savings. However, if you find yourself with a surplus of AirTags and intend to sell them, removing them from your Apple ID account before proceeding with the sale is essential.

How to reset AirTag to factory settings for others to use

When you initially set up your AirTag, it becomes intricately linked to your Apple ID, creating a secure connection that ensures it can only be utilized by you and others with authorized access. This level of association means that without resetting it, AirTag remains tethered to your "Apple ID," rendering it inaccessible to anyone else.

Fortunately, resetting an AirTag is very easy, effectively disassociating it from your Apple ID. Here's how to perform this reset:

1. Begin by Opening the Find My app on your iOS device.

2. Identify the AirTag you wish to remove from your account by selecting its name from the list.

3. Swipe upwards to reveal the complete set of AirTag settings.

4. Locate and tap on "Remove Item."

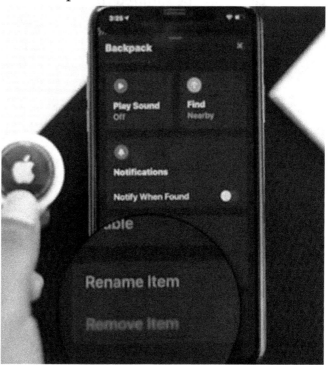

5. Confirm your decision by selecting "Remove" and then clicking "Remove" again to prompt a confirmation window.

Upon successfully completing these steps, the AirTag is effectively disengaged from your Apple ID, ready to be handed over to someone else who can set it up and associate it with their account.

However, there is a scenario in which manual resetting may be necessary. If the AirTag is not within Bluetooth range when removed from the account, it won't be able to register with a new account automatically. In such cases, a physical reset becomes essential. Here are the detailed steps to perform a physical reset:

1. Press the stainless steel support on the AirTag.
2. While pressing, rotate it counterclockwise until the lid reaches a stop point.
3. Separate the two halves of the AirTag.
4. Remove the battery.
5. Replace the battery.
6. Press the battery down firmly until you hear a distinct sound.
7. After the initial sound, repeat the process four more times, removing and replacing the battery each time while pressing it down until you hear the sound.
8. You should hear five distinct sounds during this process, confirming that the AirTag has been successfully reset.
9. After completing the reset, reattach the lid to the AirTag, aligning the three tabs on the cover with the corresponding spaces on the AirTag.
10. Press the cover down until it produces a sound, then twist it clockwise until it locks securely.

To avoid the somewhat cumbersome process of a physical reset, ensure that the person who intends to receive the AirTag is within Bluetooth range to remove it from your account properly. This straightforward approach simplifies clearing AirTag ownership and transferring it to another user, ensuring a smooth transition without needing a manual reset.

How to turn off AirTag project security alert

Apple's AirTag, the innovative object tracker, is designed to be affixed to personal items like keys, wallets, and more. The owner can effortlessly tag and monitor these possessions using their iPhone or iPad, ensuring they are never misplaced again.

Upon the successful setup of an AirTag within Apple's expansive "Find My" network, the privilege of tracking it is reserved exclusively for the owner, who can conveniently do so using their iOS device. Apple has also implemented a robust anti-tracking system to safeguard user privacy. If an anonymous AirTag is detected nearby, the individual being tracked will receive a notification, alerting them that the owner is aware of their location.

Acknowledging that some users might wish to share items tracked with an AirTag, such as a set of keys, with friends or family, Apple has provided a solution. Suppose you share an AirTag with someone within the owner's "Family Sharing" group. In that case, you can pause or deactivate the security alert, preventing family members' iPhones from being erroneously flagged as potential threats engaging in "malicious tracking."

Moreover, when an AirTag is borrowed from someone outside the "Family Sharing" network, the borrower can suspend or entirely turn off the security features on their iOS device. The subsequent steps elucidate the process for the latter option.

However, it's important to bear in mind that while the "Item Security Alert" is disabled, the owner of the anonymous object will still retain visibility of your location, and you won't receive any notifications if an unidentified item happens to be accompanying you.

Here's how to disable the "Item Security Alert":

1. Launch the "Find My" app on your iPhone or iPad.

2. Tap the "I" tab in the screen's lower right corner.
3. Toggle the switch next to "Object Security Notice."
4. Confirm your decision by selecting "Disable."

Please be aware that this setting only impacts the device you are currently using. If you wish to prevent security alerts on another device, you must repeat these steps on that particular device. This flexibility ensures that AirTag users can tailor their tracking preferences to suit their needs while respecting privacy and security.

CHAPTER 4

Tips and Tricks

When it comes to effectively tracking items, AirTag is often considered the gold standard of 21st-century baggage tracking, surpassing alternatives like the Galaxy SmartTag. However, despite its widespread acclaim, Apple's item tracker had its fair share of teething troubles, especially during its initial days.

While some users reported that their AirTags didn't work, others found the much-hyped 'Precision Search' feature inconsistent. No matter what issue you might face with your AirTag, consider these ten professional tips if it's malfunctioning or won't connect to your iPhone.

So, what could potentially cause an AirTag to misbehave? There might be more than one culprit behind the problem. While network-related issues can often be the culprits, don't overlook the possibility of a faulty battery. Moreover, incorrect configuration settings could also be to blame. Therefore, we will investigate all possible causes and apply the most effective AirTag tips and tricks accordingly.

1. **Ensure Two-Factor Authentication is Enabled:**
   To allow your AirTag to connect to your iPhone or iPad, it's essential to have two-factor authentication enabled. If you haven't already, make sure you activate 2FA on your iOS or iPadOS device.

Suppose you're encountering problems on your PC. In that case, we recommend using a dedicated tool to fix errors, safeguard against file loss, combat malware, address hardware issues, and optimize your computer for peak performance. This software can efficiently resolve PC issues and prevent future problems:

- Download the "PC Repair & Optimizer Tool (Windows 10, 8, 7, XP, Vista - Microsoft Gold Certified)."
- Click "Start Scan" to identify Windows registry problems affecting your PC.
- Click "Repair All" to resolve all issues.

To enable two-factor authentication for your Apple ID:

- Go to Settings.

○ Tap your name.

○ Select Password & Security.
○ Verify that 'two-factor authentication' is turned on. You may need to provide your phone number and answer security questions to enable 2FA for your Apple ID.

Answer security questions

Question 2 of 2:
What was the name of your best
friend as a teenager?

asif

Forgotten Answer?

2. **Confirm You're Not Using a Managed Apple ID:** Apple explicitly states that if your iOS/iPadOS device uses a Managed Apple ID, you won't be able to set up an AirTag. So, if your AirTag isn't connecting to your iPhone or iPad, ensure your device complies with this requirement.

   For those unfamiliar with the term, Managed Apple IDs are created by educational institutions like schools or universities for students' educational purposes. They are unique to each organization and distinct from your standard Apple ID.

3. **Ensure Location Services Are Enabled:** Besides being available as a standalone app, Find My also features a system-wide switch within the Settings app,

allowing you to turn it on or off based on your preferences and needs.

Here's a detailed guide on how to turn on or off Find My through the Settings app:

- Open the Settings app on your iPhone or iPad.

- Scroll down and tap on your name or Apple ID at the top of the screen.
- Now, tap on "Find My."

- Ensure the switch next to "Find My iPhone" is turned on. This switch controls the entire Find My system, including AirTags.
- You can toggle it off and on again to refresh the settings if it's already enabled.

4. **Turn Off/On Bluetooth, Wi-Fi, and Cellular Network:** Sometimes, issues with AirTag connectivity can arise due to problems with Bluetooth, Wi-Fi, or the cellular network. Resetting these wireless connections often helps resolve the problem. Follow these steps:

- Go to the Settings app on your iPhone or iPad.

- Navigate to the Wi-Fi, Bluetooth, and Mobile Data sections individually.

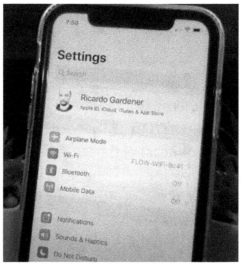

- Turn off the Wi-Fi, Cellular, and Bluetooth switches, and then restart your device.

5. **Disable/Enable Location Services:** Location Services must be enabled for AirTags to function accurately. If you're facing issues despite Location Services being on, consider disabling and re-enabling the "Location Services" switch. It can help resolve any random glitches that may have occurred.

Here's how to do it:

- Go to the Settings app on your iPhone or iPad.

- Scroll down and tap on "Privacy."

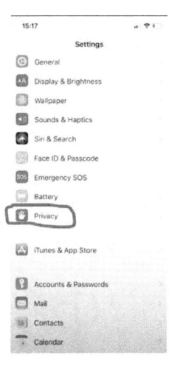

- Select "Location Services."

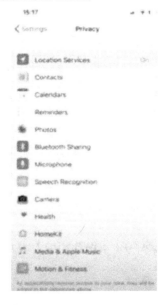

- Turn off the Location Services switch. Afterward, restart your device.

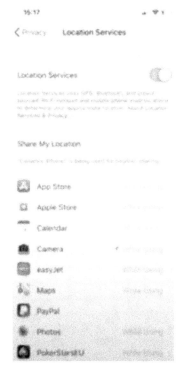

- Once your device restarts, navigate to the "Location Services" settings and turn it back on before pairing the AirTag.

6. **Troubleshooting AirTag Precision Finding:** AirTag Precision Finding allows you to accurately determine the distance and direction of a misplaced AirTag when it's within range. It leverages the U1 chip in AirTags and the latest iPhone 12 and 11 models to facilitate precise communication.

The U1 chip harnesses ultra-wideband technology and incorporates key components like the iPhone's ARKit, accelerometer, gyroscope, and camera to guide you to a lost AirTag through haptic, audio, and visual feedback.

However, it's important to note that ultra-wideband technology may be restricted in certain countries and regions. If you find Apple AirTag Precision Finding isn't working on your iPhone 12 or 11, ensure this technology isn't blocked in your location. Furthermore, ensure you've granted location access to the Find My app. To confirm and adjust these settings, follow these steps:

- Open the Settings app on your device.

- Scroll down and select "Privacy."

- Tap on "Location Services."

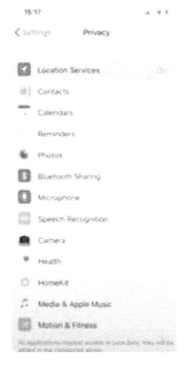

- Locate and select "Find My."

- Choose "While Using the App" and activate the "Precise Location" option.

7. **Reset Network Settings:** For AirTag to function as expected, your Wi-Fi, cellular data, and Bluetooth connections must be in working order. If there are persistent issues with AirTag connectivity, it can be helpful to reset your network settings. Here's how:

    - Open the Settings app on your iPhone or iPad.

- Scroll down and select "General."

- Scroll further down and tap on "Reset."

- Choose "Reset Network Settings."

- Enter your device passcode if prompted.

- Confirm the reset when prompted.

It will reset your network settings to their default configurations, and your device will restart. After restart, restart your Wi-Fi, cellular data, and Bluetooth connections as needed. It may help resolve any network-related issues affecting your AirTag.

8. **Reset AirTag to factory settings:** To reset your AirTag to factory settings and address potential connectivity issues, follow these steps:

   - Open the Find My app on your iPhone or iPad.

   - Navigate to the "Items" tab within the app.

- Select the specific AirTag you want to reset.
- Swipe up to access the AirTag settings.
- Tap on the "Remove Item" option at the bottom.

- Confirm your action by tapping "Remove" again.

Once you've successfully reset the AirTag, you can reconnect it to your iPhone or iPad. Hold the AirTag close to your device and tap the "Connect" button on the screen. If you have multiple AirTags and see a message stating "More than one AirTag detected," ensure that only one AirTag is near your device during this process.

9. **Remove and replace the AirTag battery:** If resetting and reconnecting the AirTag doesn't resolve the issue, you can also consider removing and replacing the AirTag. Here's how:
    - Remove the AirTag from its case or accessory.
    - Press the stainless steel back of the AirTag with two fingers.

- While pressing down, rotate counterclockwise until the lid stops rotating.
- Separate the two halves of the AirTag.
- Remove the old battery and replace it with a new CR2032 battery.

10. **Update the iPhone and iPad software:** the AirTag still doesn't work properly after battery replacement; consider checking for software updates on your iPhone or iPad. Software updates often include performance improvements and bug fixes that may address AirTag connectivity issues:

- Open the Settings app on your iPhone or iPad.

- Scroll down and select "General."

- Tap on "Software Update."

- If an update is available, download and install it.

Updating your device's software can resolve compatibility or connectivity problems with AirTag.

Reset AirTag with "Find My App"

Sure, let's dive into the world of the Find My app and understand how it plays a crucial role in troubleshooting and resetting your AirTags. Whether you're a tech enthusiast or just getting started, getting to know this handy tool is essential for resolving any AirTag-related issues.

The Find My app is like the control center for your AirTags and comes built into various Apple devices, from iPhones and iPads to MacBooks and Apple Watches. Its main job is to help you track and manage your AirTags. It's not just about finding lost items; it also allows you to reset, unpair, and fix common AirTag problems.

To reset your AirTags using the Find My app on your iPhone, open the app, go to the "Items" tab, and choose the AirTag you want to reset. Then, tap "Remove Item" and confirm. This process disconnects the AirTag from your Apple ID, preparing it for a fresh start. Android users can do the same using the Find My app through a web browser. Log in to your Apple ID on the iCloud website, find the Find iPhone section, select your AirTag, and follow the on-screen steps to remove it.

If you're using a MacBook, iPad, or Apple Watch, resetting AirTags is similar to what we discussed earlier. Just ensure your devices have the latest software updates for the Find My app to work its magic.

What if you don't have a compatible device to reset AirTags? You can borrow a friend's Apple device, visit an Apple Store, or contact Apple Support for help. The Find My app also doubles as a troubleshooting tool. It can guide you through issues like connectivity problems, firmware updates, and battery changes.

In a nutshell, the Find My app is your go-to for solving AirTag issues. Knowing how it works empowers you to take charge and make the most out of your AirTags. We'll explore more about specific reset methods, troubleshooting tricks, and the cool features of this app in the upcoming chapters.

If you're new to the world of technology and have recently acquired AirTags, you're in the right place for a step-by-step guide on resetting them. In this subchapter, we'll walk you through resetting AirTags using the Find My app on various devices, including iPhones, Android devices, MacBooks, iPads, and Apple Watches. We'll also cover how to reset AirTags without a compatible device, perform a factory reset, and unpair them from your Apple ID. Additionally, we'll provide troubleshooting tips for common issues that crop up during the reset process.

Resetting your AirTags using the Find My app is a straightforward process that can be completed in simple steps. Here's the breakdown:

1. Open the Find My app on your device. If you don't have it installed, you can easily download it from the App Store or Google Play Store.

2. Sign in with your Apple ID or the account linked to your AirTags.

3. Navigate to the "Items" tab within the app to access your list of AirTags.

4. Select the specific AirTag you wish to reset from the list.
5. Scroll down and tap on the "Remove Item" option.

6. Confirm the action by tapping "Remove" or "Unpair," depending on your device.

7. Your AirTag will now be reset and ready for a fresh setup.

There's no need to fret if you find yourself without a compatible device to reset your AirTags. You can manually reset them by removing the battery and reinserting it after a few seconds. This action effectively restores the AirTag to its factory settings, giving you a clean slate to work with.

Factory reset your Apple AirTag

When you connect your AirTag with your iPhone, it becomes linked to your Apple ID. If you ever plan to hand it off to someone else or sell it, you'll want to ensure it's returned to its original factory settings. Resetting your AirTag is straightforward, especially when a Bluetooth connection is readily available. Furthermore, you can employ useful tips and tricks to make this operation seamless.

Factory resetting your AirTags proves valuable when you encounter functionality hiccups or decide to disassociate them from your Apple ID. In this subchapter, we will guide you through resetting AirTags on various devices, including iPhones, Android devices, MacBooks, iPads, and Apple Watches. Moreover, we'll delve into resetting AirTags without a compatible device and address common troubleshooting challenges during this process.

You can follow these simple steps when resetting your AirTags on an iPhone.

Launch the Find My app and tap on the "Items" tab.

Locate the AirTag you wish to reset, tap it, and then choose "Remove Item."

Confirm your choice by tapping on "Remove." This sequence of actions will effectively restore the AirTag to its factory settings and detach it from your Apple ID.

Android device users have a slightly different process for resetting AirTags. Access the Find My app on a compatible Android device or through a web browser. Sign in with your Apple ID, proceed to the "Items" section, spot the AirTag, and select "Remove Item." Confirm your decision, and the AirTag will be reset.

MacBook, iPad, and Apple Watch users can reset their AirTags through the Find My app. Open the app on your device, navigate to the "Items" tab, locate the AirTag, and opt for "Remove Item." Verify your choice, and the AirTag will be returned to its factory settings.

But what if you lack a compatible device for resetting your AirTags? No need to fret; there's a solution. You can borrow a friend's iPhone, iPad, or another compatible device, log in to the Find My app using your Apple ID, and execute the steps outlined to reset the AirTag.

In some instances, you may face issues during the reset process. For example, the AirTag might not be detected, or the reset may fail. In such cases, ensure your device is operating on the latest operating system and that the Find My app is up to date. A device restart can also work wonders. If the problem persists, don't hesitate to contact Apple support for further assistance.

By understanding the nuances of factory resetting AirTags and tackling common troubleshooting hurdles, you'll be well-equipped to manage and resolve any issues that come your way effectively. Remember, resetting AirTags offers a clean slate, addressing connectivity and pairing concerns and ensuring your peace of mind regarding their performance.

Step-by-Step Guide to Factory Reset Airtags

Common Problems while Factory Resetting AirTags

Resetting AirTags is a valuable troubleshooting technique, serving various purposes, including preparing them for resale. However, those new to the world of technology often grapple with common issues during this process. This dedicated section will delve into these complications and offer step-by-step solutions for resetting AirTags across different devices. If you're an iPhone user, the process involves ensuring you're running the latest iOS version, accessing the Find My app, and carefully following on-screen instructions.

For Android users, it's essential to note that AirTags can only be reset using Apple devices, so borrowing a friend's iPhone or visiting an Apple Store may be necessary. The process aligns closely with the iPhone method on a MacBook, iPad, or Apple Watch, but on an Apple Watch, you'll need an alternative Apple device. When resetting AirTags without a compatible device, consider borrowing one or seek support from an Apple Store or Apple Support. Remember that resetting AirTags disassociates them from your Apple ID, making them ready for use by someone else, and troubleshooting assistance is readily available.

Troubleshooting Issues with Find My App

The Find My app, a potent tool for tracking and managing your AirTags, is undoubtedly valuable. However, like all technological marvels, it is only partially devoid of its fair share of challenges. In this dedicated section, we'll embark on a journey to uncover the common predicaments you might encounter while navigating the terrain of the Find My app. Moreover, we'll arm you with comprehensive step-by-step solutions to effortlessly troubleshoot and resolve these potential stumbling blocks.

Among the chief difficulties beginners often face is resetting AirTags through the Find My app. For iPhone users, the process is a straightforward endeavor. You open the Find My app, locate your AirTag, and initiate the reset by tapping it. Next, scroll down and select the enticing "Remove Item" option. Subsequently, adhere to the on-screen prompts to execute a seamless reset.

For those wielding Android devices, the procedure possesses a slight variation. Within the Find My app, pinpoint your AirTag and then gracefully tap on the dots accompanying it. Select the "Remove Item" option from the ensuing drop-down menu and follow the instructions, ensuring a pristine reset.

MacBook, iPad, and Apple Watch users are in luck, as the steps for resetting an AirTag closely mirror those outlined earlier. By initiating the Find My app on your respective device, selecting the target AirTag, and gently clicking on the "Remove Item" option, you pave the way for a harmonious reset experience. Your adherence to the on-screen guidance will render the process effortlessly navigable.

However, what if the fates have conspired against you, and a compatible device for resetting your AirTag remains elusive? Fear not, for a solution lies within your grasp. You can execute an AirTag reset by simply pressing and holding the button on the AirTag itself. The sound that ensues will act as your guiding star, signifying the commencement of the reset process. Once you hear the subsequent chime, you can rest assured that your

AirTag has been successfully reset, even without a companion device.

Yet, challenges may arise in the grand tapestry of technological endeavors, and your journey within the Find My app may hit a bump. If such a problem occurs, you fret not. The path to resolution begins with ensuring that your Find My app is up-to-date, boasting the latest version available. A quick trip to your device's app store should set things right. Additionally, it's prudent to scrutinize your internet connection, as a less-than-optimal link may introduce hiccups into the app's operation. Lastly, consider the simple yet effective act of restarting your device. Sometimes, a fresh start can be the key to unlocking your troubleshooting success.

Manually reset AirTag

If you find yourself outside the Bluetooth range of your AirTag when attempting to remove it from your account, it won't complete the deregistration process. In such cases, you'll have to reset the AirTag manually. It involves a series of steps to ensure it's wiped clean and ready for a new owner.

To manually reset your AirTag, begin by pressing on the stainless steel side. While pressing down, rotate the cover counterclockwise until it stops turning.

Next, gently separate the two parts of the AirTag and remove the battery. After that, reinsert the battery and press it down until you hear a distinct sound. You'll want to repeat this process four times – yes, you'll have to remove and replace the battery, pressing it down until you hear five beeps.

Once you've completed these steps, reattach the metal cover to the AirTag in its original position.

Align the three tabs on the cover with the corresponding locations on the device tracker, and press down until it clicks into place. Finish by turning it clockwise to secure it firmly. Congratulations, you've now successfully reset your AirTag manually.

This same method can also be used to disable an AirTag that's been traveling with you and set it up as your own. However, manually resetting an AirTag can be a bit time-consuming, so always ensure that the person who initially gave you the AirTag has deleted it from their account while the device tracker is still within Bluetooth range.

Turn off the AirTag project security warning

In the interest of security, iOS 14 introduced a crucial feature that permits only AirTag owners to use the 'I Found' app to track their devices.

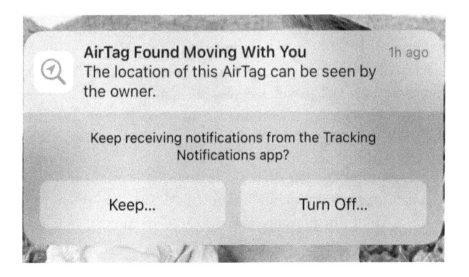

Additionally, it includes an anti-tracking system that will issue a warning if an unfamiliar AirTag appears to be moving with you. This notification is a thoughtful safety measure, informing you that the AirTag owner can access your location.

Your current location can be seen by the owner of this AirTag

This AirTag may be attached to an item you are borrowing. If this AirTag is not familiar to you, you can disable it and stop sharing your location.

But what if you want to share your AirTag tracking information with trusted friends or family members without compromising your security? You may be reluctant to turn off this essential security feature, and that's perfectly understandable. The good news is that iOS provides a way to temporarily pause these security alerts so your iPhone or iPad won't repeatedly detect unfamiliar AirTags.

It's important to note that while Item Safety Warnings are paused, the owner of an unknown AirTag can track your whereabouts. Furthermore, you won't receive alerts if you move in the opposite direction of that unknown item while it's in your vicinity.

To pause Item Safety Warnings, open the Find My app on your iPhone or iPad and navigate to the 'I' tab. You'll find an option to toggle off 'Item Safety Warnings.'

Once you do this, a popup notification will appear on your screen, cautioning you that 'the holder of an unknown AirTag will be able to see your location, and you will no longer receive warnings when an unknown item is found moving with you.' To proceed, tap on 'Deactivate' to authorize this action.

CONCLUSION

A irTag is an innovative device that has revolutionized the way we monitor our personal possessions. It has offered a seamless and effective solution to the age-old issue of lost items, whether it's keys, wallets, luggage, or even pets. AirTag utilizes advanced technology to enable tracking of items anytime and anywhere. This book has dived into the history, creation, and deployment of AirTag, as well as its influence on our daily routines. From the advantages of its ultra wideband technology to its privacy features, AirTag has proved to be a game-changing addition to the world of tracking gadgets. As we increasingly depend on technology to simplify our lives, AirTag serves as a testament to the potential of innovation in transforming the way we live.

www.ingramcontent.com/pod-product-compliance
Lightning Source LLC
LaVergne TN
LVHW051708050326
832903LV00032B/4078